THE TEN COMMANDMENTS OF CHILD SUPPORT

Learn From My Mistakes
Save Money, Time and Heartache

Written By: SIR ROD PATTERSON
Edited By: Gregory Futrell

THE TEN COMMANDMENTS OF
CHILD SUPPORT
Copyright © 2014 by Sir Rod Patterson

CONTENTS

FIRST THINGS FIRST 5
DEDICATION 6
FORWARD 8
POWER OF CHOICE 10
CHILD SUPPORT 11

COMMANDMENT I 13
Thou Shall Not Run, Hide or Ignore

COMMANDMENT II 18
Thou Shall Know The Game

COMMANDMENT III 22
Thou Shall Get A DNA Test

COMMANDMENT IV 25
Thou Shall Be Legal Father

COMMANDMENT V 29
Thou Shall Get Visitation

COMMANDMENT VI 32
Thou Shall Pay Something

COMMANDMENT VII 35
Thou Shall Man Up

COMMANDMENT VIII 38
Thou Shall Handle Thy Business

COMMANDMENT IX 42
Thou Shall Keep It Real

COMMANDMENT X 45
*Thou Shall Know It's For
The Children*

14 TIPS FOR SURVIVING 49
MY RUNNING STORY 74
THE SOLUTION 90
VOCABULARY 94

FIRST THINGS FIRST

My lawyers are insisting that I inform you that "The Ten Commandments of Child Support" isn't meant as a replacement for legal advice. Neither is it intended to take the place of legal representation. Because every situation is different, you should always seek guidance from an attorney or government office to provide you with specific information that can better fit your situation or problem. So, now that we've gotten that out of the way, read and learn from lessons it took me over 30 years to learn.

DEDICATION

I'd like to dedicate this book to the three women, in my life, that have shaped and molded me into the man I am, today. First and most important is my mother, Ollie Patterson. You've been gone for over 13 years. However, not a day goes by that one of your many life lessons doesn't cross my mind. It was your love, kindness and patience, with a difficult child, that was so awesome. You allowed me to be me, without judgment. In addition, you always displayed so much love towards me. I miss you, Ma!

Secondly, I dedicate this book to my wife of 20 years, Avias. Through the good and the bad times, you have been there, by my side, all the way. Most women would have packed up and left me with all my child support issues, hang-ups and drama. Why you took a chance on me, I'll never know. Thank you for your patience, belief in me and for blessing me with a son. I am, truly, a blessed man!

Last, to the mother of my two oldest children, Cheryl, I can truly say, today, thank you for holding me to the fire. What I thought was a curse, years ago, was truly a blessing. Looking back over the many years, I'm in awe of our perseverance, strength and accomplishments. We were just teens when our first child was born. You had just turned 17, and I had only been 18 for three days. Given our surroundings, we should've just been another sad statistic. However, through God's grace and mercy, we overcame. Now, you have a doctorate degree. Our daughter is a Broadway and movie actress and I'm an author and one of the top motivational speakers in the nation. None of our accomplishments would've happened without our journey. So, again, thank you for holding me to the fire. That fire refined, purified and has put me in the position that I'm in, today. It is a position enabling me to reach thousands of absentee parents and teach through real life lessons.

Again, thank you all!

FORWARD

No Need To Hunt Me Down :o)

Okay, women before you hunt me down, tar and feather me, this book isn't about not paying child support. It's about empowering absent parents to take responsibility for their children and/or adult actions. My goal is to, hopefully, get these fathers to step up to the plate and eliminate the need for a court to force them to pay. Once that's accomplished, there's no longer a need for child support, because they're addressing their RESPONSIBILITIES. This book comes from a voice of experience. Having been in the child support system for over 26 years and having to pay from $72 to $1,200 monthly, I feel I've become an expert. At times, I was that deadbeat dad; and, at other times, I was a caring father; giving my last dime to my children. Whether I was either of those extremes, child support was the one thing that stayed a constant thorn in my side. This book and all the information, within it, isn't for the deadbeats. For they're the ones that child support was made for and who've made it hard for everyone else. The system assumes you are a deadbeat, first. This book is for anyone that wants to do the right thing. Forget your past! It's never too late to reframe from the "Stop Running" syndrome and become "Mr. or Ms. Responsible." Again, I was both "Mr. Deadbeat" and "Mr. Responsible" at different periods in my life, from age 17 until age 42. It has been a very long journey dealing with the child support system. Nevertheless, I will share with you some of my personal stories and at the same time hope that men and women learn from my experiences to save time, pain, money and heartache.

POWER OF CHOICE
50¢ or $54,288…Your Choice

I need you to remember this number, $54,288. Let me spell it out for you: fifty-four thousand two hundred eighty-eight dollars. This number is important because this is the least amount of child support you will be able to pay at minimum wage, for 18 years, for one child. That number only goes up if you make more money and if you have multiple children. Now, that's only child support. I'm sure you can understand that it will cost a lot more once you factor in doctor visits, school supplies, birthdays, Christmas presents, swimming lessons, clothes and piano lessons, etc. I want to be clear on the cost and responsibility for raising a child. However, if you're a deadbeat dad, you probably wouldn't be concerned about that number, nor the responsibilities of a child. Men, responsibility begins with you; not the woman. I tell this to my sons and I'll share this advice with you. No matter what a woman tells you, wrap it up! It will help you avoid a lot of financial headaches and pain that come with an unplanned pregnancy. So, I'll state this once more: a 50¢ condom or $54,288. The choice is yours.

CHILD SUPPORT
Two Scary Words

A man can be a man's man. He can be tall as Shaq and weigh 480 lbs. It's funny how two little words can make that manly man run trembling in fear like a little girl. The two scary words are CHILD SUPPORT.

The definition for Child Support reads:
Court-ordered payments; typically made by a noncustodial divorced parent, to support one's minor children

Now, the definition doesn't seem to be that scary. After all, who would be afraid of helping take care of their offspring? So, why are men so afraid of those words? It's simple. The main reason is because of the information men receive regarding child support as well as the method in which they're receiving it. It's mostly coming from the evening news or newspapers about deadbeat dads getting arrested. In addition, they'd hear about some guy having his bank account or his taxes frozen, as well as all his money being taken by the evil child support monster. Perhaps it's also hearing his girlfriend or wife threatening to put him on child support, if he doesn't do what she asks of him or behave in a certain way. With understanding, the "child support monster" loses some of its bite. Most couples, upon breaking up, can work together and work out some kind of agreement for the future care of their children. Now, if that agreement is breached and the custodial parent can't get the absent parent's help in supporting the children, the custodial parent can turn over their situation to the state, to enforce support. At that point, the state will ask for all custodial and noncustodial financial records, back accounts, investments, 401k, etc. Depending on how much or how little you make will determine what child support amount will be set. Now, if the noncustodial parent pays that amount on time, he or she will never hear from the courts. However, what happens if the noncustodial refuses to pay? Well, the state or judge won't come knocking on the door asking you "Where's the money?" The state courts will contract out collection agencies to do their dirty work, for them. These collection agencies are kind of like the collection agencies you deal with when you don't pay your credit card on time, except these collection agencies have power. They have the power to make you comply with the court's orders. A lot of bad things start to happen, such as wage garnishments, tax liens, drivers and business licenses suspension; even jail. All the stuff you hear on the evening news and newspapers about deadbeat dads tend to occur. My goal, with this book, is to do away with all these fears and free men from anyone controlling them with the words "child support."

"You cannot escape the responsibility of tomorrow by evading it today."
~ Abraham Lincoln

COMMANDMENT I

Now, I know you are going to be surprised. However, believe it or not, the child support system isn't to be taken personal. It is not out to wreak havoc or destroy you. The child support system is just that, a SYSTEM. It's kind of like the IRS. It's just not as complicated. Similarly, both systems are broken and have caused havoc and destroyed many lives, when men don't pay. In other words, it's not personal. It's just business. You, your ex-wife, girlfriend, and child are all just numbers in the system. As a matter of fact, if you, your ex-wife or girlfriend entered the child support system and never had any issues, such as missed payments, the system wouldn't know either of you existed.

Most men, myself included, fight the system and lose. It took me almost 16 years to figure that out. Once I figured it out, I started to look at it differently, almost with pity. You see, the business of child support is a very sad business to be involved in. It's a business that deals with people at very inopportune or bad times in their lives. Most of the time, it's after a bad break up or divorce. To top it off, there's the issue of the child. A lot of the time, if the break up is because of the man, some women will use the child and the child support system like a weapon against the man. When

COMMANDMENT I

that happens, I believe four things may occur: 1). The man may verbally or physically attack the woman. 2). The child is hurt or neglected. 3). He verbally attacks the system and people within the system. 4). He simply runs or walks away.

Way to often, men tend to take the latter choice, running or walking away. Sticking your head in the sand or ignoring the situation is really not an option. If you didn't know there was not a "statue of limitations" in most states for collecting child support; meaning that your children can be grown and you still will owe the mother and state, you know now. I'm telling you this because I experienced this, first-hand. My daughter is 28; son is 25; and, I'm still paying arrears to the state of Georgia. So, since your only real choice is to play the game, you may as well play the game right.

At one point in my life, when I was younger, I didn't take child support, the child support office, system or any of the enforcers serious. I felt like I had been lied to. When I was first interviewed by my child support case-worker, she made it seem as if I could go to the office anytime I wanted and get my child support reduced, if there was a change in my income. However, the truth of the matter is, it was a long and

COMMANDMENT I

very complex process to get the rate lowered or increased. After I figured out I had been tricked, I did what a lot of men tend to do. I ran, hid and stuck my head in the sand, hoping that it would go away. However, it never did.

I ran for eight years. I would, simply, quit my job whenever they would find me. What I mean by "find me" is when child support would garnish my paycheck. I had it down to a science. I knew it would take child support enforcement about a year to catch up with me/find me. Since all the jobs I worked were dead-end jobs, back then, I had no problem quitting them. I had no idea this would catch up with me, one day, but it did.

COMMANDMENT II

THOU SHALL KNOW THE GAME

" You have to learn the rules of the game. And then you have to play better than anyone else."
~ Albert Einstein

COMMANDMENT II

Okay, to play the game right is really to know your rights. Contrary to your beliefs or what you may have heard, fathers and/or absentee parents do have rights, and I would wager that you would be pleasantly surprised to know you have a lot of rights. For me, playing the game meant I would tell the child support office whatever they wanted to hear. One of the ways to play the game was to dress down when going to meet with my caseworker. I noticed how they'd watch what kind of clothes and shoes I was wearing. I'd take off any jewelry before they questioned me about it. In other words, it was hard to convince them that I didn't have any money, while wearing a thousand dollars worth of gold or clothes. I've seen a lot of guys get caught like this.

Another way I played "The Game" was by working low paying jobs to keep my payments down. I found out that if I made too much money, child support would take 28% off the gross income, not the net. In addition, the government would tax 33% of the gross income. That's half your pay, already. Here, in Georgia, where I currently live, there is a 6% state tax. So, even more of my money was gone. After working a 40-hour workweek and having everything taken out, I had about $27 left to my name. I had no choice but to play the game. I was

COMMANDMENT II

playing the game but hadn't the slightest idea what the real game was. I guess I was lucky I landed a job as a bellman.

As a bellman, I was paid mainly with tips. This job put me in control of my income. I kept the tip money for bills and living. That left child support to garnish only the small paycheck I was getting. This way, I didn't raise any red flags. The bonus was I really liked the job. I ended up working as a bellman for over 6 years. I was also able to go back to school to study graphic design. I was making up rules to the game as I went along. Nevertheless, I was now in the system; and, in a small way, I felt like I was a slave to the game.

*"Get up, stand up, Stand up for your rights.
Get up, stand up, Don't give up the fight."*
*~ **Bob Marley***

COMMANDMENT III

You know the old saying "Mama's Baby, Daddy's Maybe." That is a true phrase. There is nothing sadder than hearing that a man did the right thing; was there for his child for eighteen years; paid and loved his child, just to find out that he's not the child's biological father. To add to the injury, you can't even sue to get your money back. In the law's eyes, you assumed the roll of the official father of that child.

Guys, you have to be smart. Don't just take her word. Think about it. Do you think she would really tell you there's a small chance it might be another man's baby? Get a DNA test on every child! It's worth the cost and peace of mind.

"I cannot think of any need in childhood as strong as the need for a father's protection."
*~ **Sigmund Freud***

COMMANDMENT IV

The thing you have to establish, first, is the position of power, which is to become the legal father. The legal father has a lot of rights. As a matter of fact, you have just as many rights as the legal mother. The legal father can change the child's name. He has the right to visitation, as well as where the child will go to school. In addition, the legal mother can't move out of state without the legal father's consent. Most men are not aware of this. To assume the role of just the biological father is not enough. That father, without documentation, doesn't have any rights, under the law, until he becomes the legal father.

Let me give you an example of a situation how a child can have three fathers:

Sally is married to Fred. Sally has had a short fling/affair with Dave. Dave breaks it off with Sally and finds a new girlfriend. Sally is hurt. So, she finds Kevin, a side guy to get over Dave. Sally finds out she's pregnant. She's not sure who the father is. So, Sally lies and tells Dave he's the father, since Fred had a vasectomy. She tells Fred, her husband, she is pregnant and he assumes responsibility. She never tells him that it might be Kevin's. Kevin was just a one-night-stand used to get over Dave. Eventually, Dave steps up to the plate and start giving Sally money for the child

So, at this point, Sally's child has 3 fathers:

Fred (legal father)
Dave (financial father)
Kevin (biological father)

If Sally was to die in a car crash and Dave or Kevin wanted to get custody of the child, they probably wouldn't have a snowball chance in hell because Fred's position as the legal father out weighs everything. The law is simple. Any child that comes out of a man's wife, legally, belongs to that wife's husband. Now, he can choose to give up his rights and hand the child over to the biological father. However, if he doesn't, you will have to seek and resolve your rights in court.

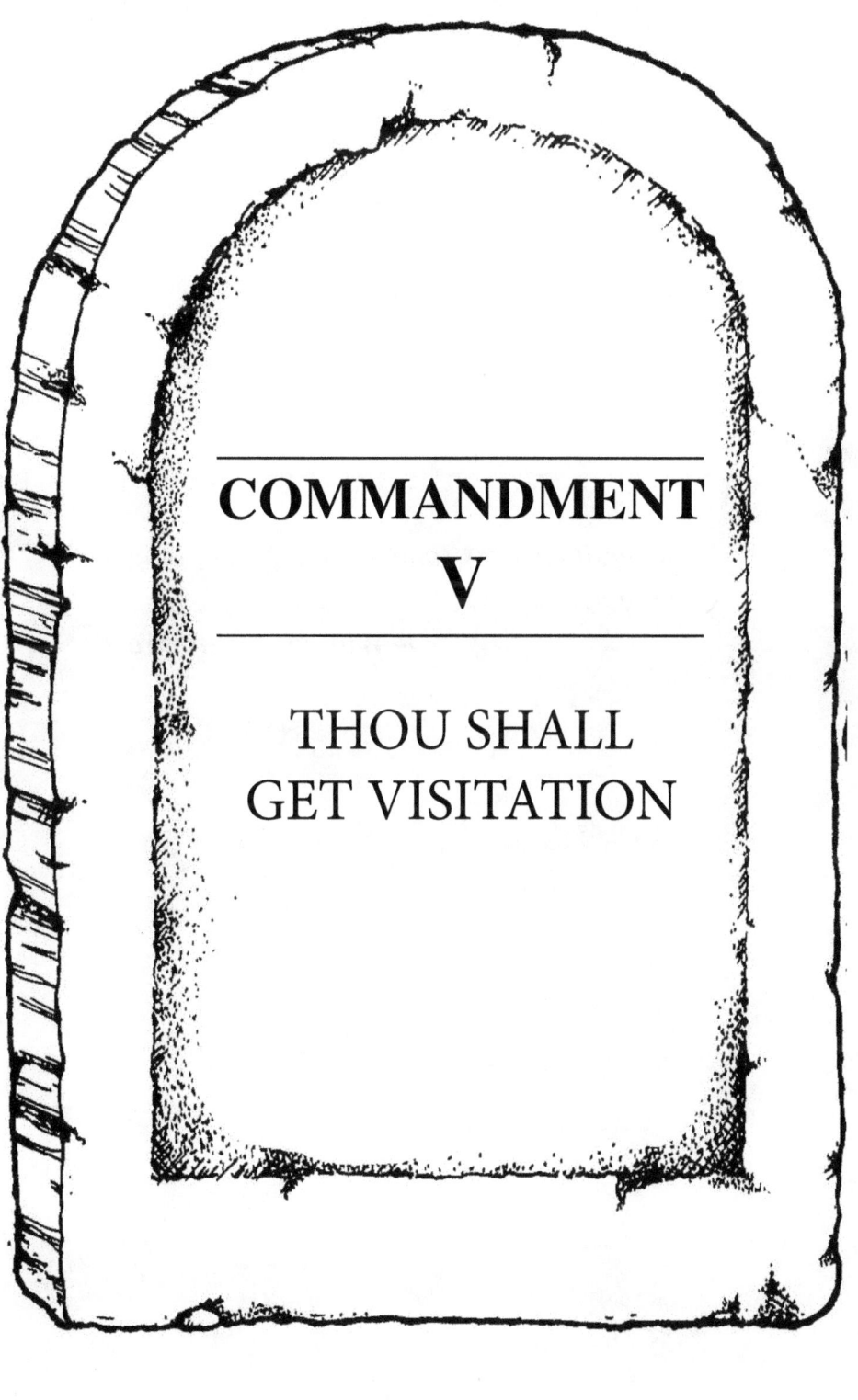

"Adversity causes some men to break; others to break records."

*~ **William Arthur Ward***

COMMANDMENT V

This is the order in which you should do things:

1. DNA
2. Legal Father
3. Visitation

Seeking an order of visitation is important. It makes you look good to the judge. More importantly, your child or children need more then just money and material things from you. More valuable then anything to them is TIME with you. And, that's Priceless. If the mother doesn't honor it, she can be arrested. Likewise, if you don't honor it and don't pick up your child when you're suppose to, or vice versa, you can be arrested as well. So, make sure you set realistic dates and times that will work for you and the child. Weekends, summers and holidays will all be worked out in the visitation order. In addition, make sure you spell out what happens with your child support payments if you have the child for an extended period of time.

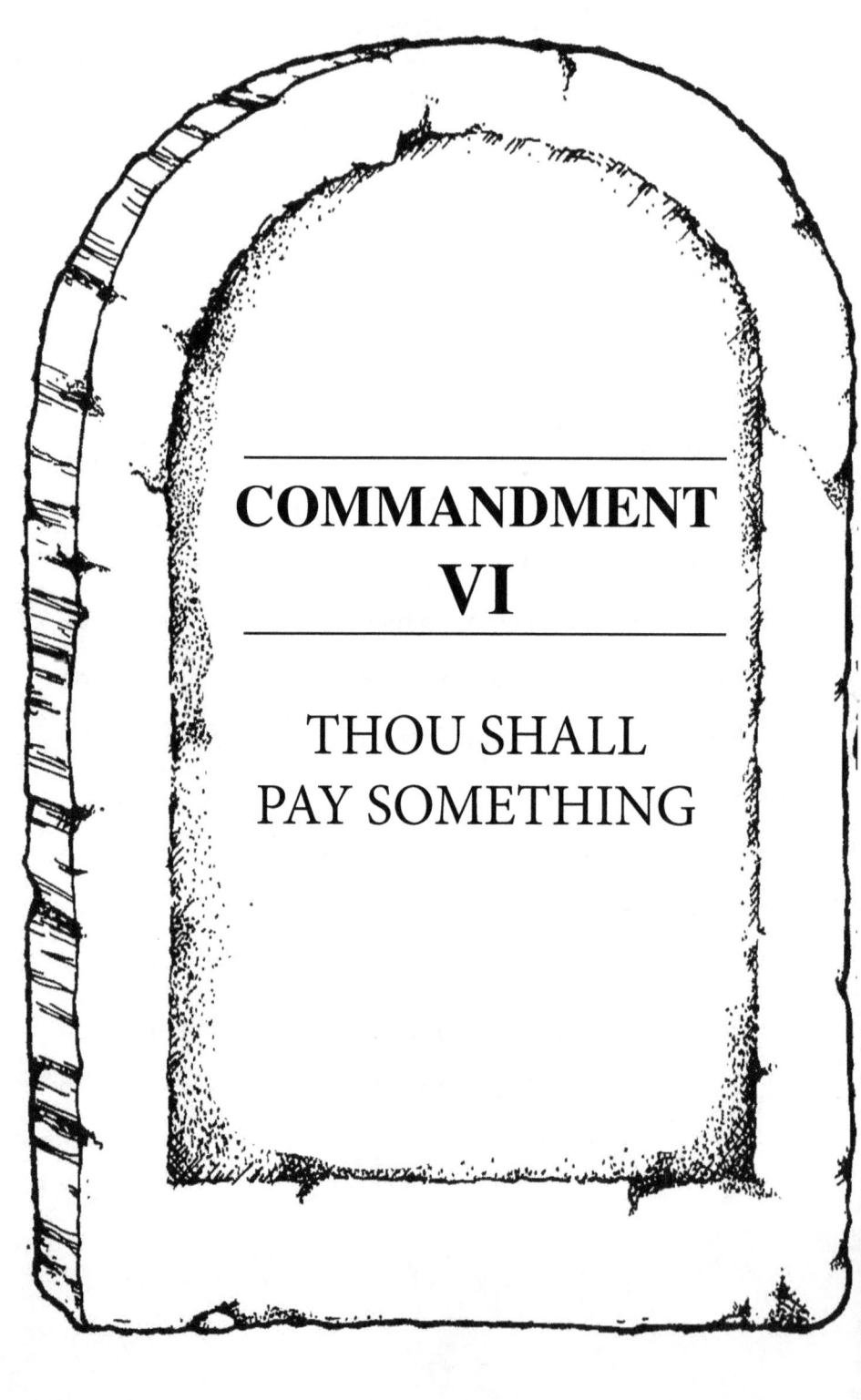

"Mistakes are part of the dues one pays for a full life."

*~ **Sophia Loren***

COMMANDMENT VI

I tell this to men all the time: PAY SOMETHING EVERY MONTH!!! I was like most men. If I couldn't make a full child support payment, I wouldn't pay anything. That was a BIG MISTAKE! I don't care if you can only pay $5.00. Send it in! Your caseworkers/ child support collectors will scream and moan. However, send it anyway. Here's why you need to think about the judges point-of-view: If the judge is looking at two cases, and one happens to be yours, where you haven't made any payments cause you didn't have the full amount; and, there's a guy on the other side who is also behind on payments, just like you, but the judge sees that he's been trying, by making small payment of $10, $40, $15, $5, etc, who do you think the judge will give a break to? In other words, even if you can't make a full payment, PAY SOMETHING!!!

COMMANDMENT VII

THOU SHALL MAN UP

"A successful man is one who can lay a firm foundation with the bricks others have thrown at him."

~ David Brinkley

COMMANDMENT VII

Don't let any one fool you. A father figure is needed in a child's life. No one can replace you, the father. Women try raising children alone, all the time. However, they can no more replace a man, no more than a man can replace a woman. Men tend to give up way to soon in fighting for their children. They let the baby mamas and the courts chase them away. They just plain give up because there's just too much drama. MAN UP!!! If you don't fight to be in your child's life, who will? I'm giving you the tools and the wisdom in this book to help you take your rightful position. No one said it's going to be easy. If you're looking for easy, you're going to be waiting a very long time. When it comes to child support and legal matters, concerning your child or children, you need to play chess not checkers. I understand that your case may be the most unique case ever seen in the world. I know because that's how I felt, at one time. I'm sure there's someone going through the same challenges you are. The trick is how you deal with the challenges.

"There are no secrets to success. It is the result of preparation, hard work, and learning from failure."

~ Colin Powell

COMMANDMENT VIII

I've put a lot of thought into this. I know this might not work for everyone. However, entrepreneurship is an option. That's right, you should start your own business. If you're self-employed, you don't have to worry about half of your paycheck being garnished. You can control your books so you know how much child support you will owe. I know it is easier said then done. Trust me, if you really want peace of mind over your finances, start your own business. It really doesn't take a lot of money. Start small and build it up.

The problem with working a regular nine-to-five is every few years your child support can be raised if you have an increase in pay. Also, child support is on your gross pay, not your net pay; meaning, they will take out up to 28% of your pay off the top. Then, the government will tax you on the gross at 28%. I've worked a 40-hour week and brought home $130 out of $600. The only way you can survive is to work two jobs or start your own business. It took awhile for me to figure out that you can't work a low paying, regular nine-to-five if you are a part of the child support system. What I found out, for me, is that child support is like another major tax on your paycheck. Depending on how many children you have and what state you live in, it can be 15% to 28% of your

COMMANDMENT VIII

gross income. Then, you still owe the regular federal and state taxes of your gross. Long story short, after child support and taxes, you're left with almost nothing. So, you can work two jobs, or do like I did and start your own business.

Wait! I almost forgot! Another way to control your earnings is to work a job that pays mostly in cash, such as bartending, waiting tables, or working as a bellman. If you think about it, those jobs are kind of like owning your own business. My goal is not to help anyone avoid paying child support. My hope is to give you some relief from the pressure. I think relief will give someone who is trying to do the right thing, hope. With hope, it's my belief, that it will only make things better for all involved; most importantly, your child or children.

"Honesty is more than not lying. It is truth telling, truth speaking, truth living, and truth loving."
~ James E. Faust

COMMANDMENT IX

Be real to and for your child, at all times; meaning, don't lie to them or mislead them. Under no conditions, should you talk down to their mother. There is an old saying, "More is caught than taught." The truth will come to light. It always does. Try to make your child's world as peaceful as possible.

"We can easily forgive a child who is afraid of the dark; the real tragedy of life is when men are afraid of the light."

~ Sigmund Freud

COMMANDMENT X

I can't say it any clearer than this: It is not your child's fault! This is easier said than understood. Somehow, the lines get blurred. This is not just for the fathers. The mothers sometime will use the children as a tool to manipulate the fathers. By the same token, some fathers don't see their children or may stand the children up to get some kind of reaction from the mother. Either way, neither father or mother is right. I make it a rule to try not to say anything negative about the mothers of my children. Though it gets hard, sometimes. I mean it can get really, really hard!

Now, if a parent is causing harm to a child, it's your responsibility to report it or take the proper measures. I have to say "proper measures" because some men think the laws of the land will change just because they are angry or upset. My advice is to filter as much negativity out of your child's life as possible. Kids have enough to deal with in life, anyway. Some advice my father told me once when I was having problems with my ex was, "You don't have to say anything bad about the mother, because one day the kids will see for themselves. It's just a matter of time." So, be a role model for your kids and make them your primary focus. Everything else will fall in place. I promise you it will.

COMMANDMENT X

I have covered some of my personal experiences dealing with the child support system. I've also tried to get you to think of things from a business perspective. At the end of the day, it's all about the children. I've found that in most cases, all sides want what's best for the children. Unfortunately, the very reason the system was made ends up only hurting those children. I want you to keep that in mind before you launch your battle against your ex, or the system.

14 TIPS FOR SURVIVING THE SYSTEM

The tips you are about to read are things I've learned regarding the child support system. Any one of these tips could be commandments in their own right. I believe they will save you time, energy, money and heartache. If applied with the previous "Ten Commandments of Child Support," you will never be labeled a deadbeat dad. These tips are my life-learned advice.

TIP 1 **Know The Vocabulary**

I can't emphasize enough how important it is to know the vocabulary. I can remember being stressed out not knowing what was going on when the lawyers started with all the "thee's and thou's." Once I started to understand the terminology, my eyes were opened and I, at least, knew what I didn't want to happen. I then started to figure out a way to avoid potential problems. So, I've added a few commonly used terms you should know. They're in the back of the book. You will see some of these words in documents and other paperwork that you have or may receive from your lawyer, court orders, summons to court, as well as the child support office. These are only some basic terms. I'd advise you to go online and familiarize yourself with as many as you can.

TIP 2 **Know Your Rights**

Yes, you have rights. Funny thing is I didn't know this, at the time! I felt like it was me against the world. I wasted so much time running and trying to hide from the problem. I was like an ostrich with its head in the sand, with the rest of its body, totally, exposed. Years later, I found out I had rights. So, that is one of the first things you are going to need to know, your rights. I'm not sure what state you're in. However, there are some basic rights you should be aware of.

They are:

- Right to be involved in the child's life
- Request custody of the child
- Request child support if you're granted custody
- Visitation with the child, with no interference from the custodial parent

It is up to you to demand your due process and/or your rights under your state's laws.

TIP 3 **Create A Paper Trail**

If you're in the middle of a bad break-up and your ex is using the system against you, becoming legal can start the cards in your favor. Once you're documented as the legal father and have visitation rights, if your ex tries to prohibit you from seeing your child, you can call the police. If she threatens, hit you, or breaks something of yours, I encourage you to call the police. Get a police report for every incident. This will help you in court. You see, women do this all the time. Just what do you think a judge would think if he or she saw you behind on child support, as well as with a pile of police reports associated with you? I think you get the picture! So, start your own paper trail. This doesn't mean create situations. What it mean is don't just ignore them when they happen.

TIP 4 Stay Low-Key

Try hard to stay low-key. I know it's been said the best revenge is success. However, that's not the case in the child support game. This is a very different kind of game. Remember the old saying "More Money, More Problems?" Success could mean the death of your finances. It's best to be low-key. You have to fight off the urge to showboat. It is hard to convince a judge that you can't pay your child support payments when you have a new car, Rolex as well as an apartment on the beach. Live below your means. This doesn't mean you have to live like a vagrant. A low-key life style will save you a lot of money in the long run. I remember when I was asked to come meet with my child support worker for being behind on my payments. I was providing a laundry list of excuses why payments were late. The caseworker wasn't listening to a word I had to say. She cut me off mid sentence and said, "nice shoes," while she pointed at my new Nikes. Then, she said, "nice watch." I realized she was calculating what I was wearing. Afterwards, she told me to sell my watch and the shoes and make my payment within 3 days.

TIP 5 Know That Life Isn't Fair

What is fair? Well, if you haven't figured it out yet, you will, someday. Life isn't fair! The best thing you can hope for is what is best for your child or children. Now, because you and your ex have split and child support is involved, it is safe for me to say that there isn't a perfect solution. In a perfect world, there's no divorce, and parents stay together forever. In the perfect divorce, you and your ex would just separate, never argue, and only positive things are said about each other. No one takes a dime of anyone's money. The only focus is to love your child or children. Yeah, right! If that world existed, would you be reading this book? Anyway, it's not a perfect world; and, every situation is different. So, that is why we have the child support system.

Believe it or not, I think the child support system is fair in that it treats all people the same. However, the wealthy can afford to hire lawyers to manipulate the system to work in their favor. Unfortunately, the other 99% of us can't afford such representation. That's why I hope this book will be a useful tool to help you navigate through your child support woes.

TIP 6 Keep A Business State Of Mind

It may sound somewhat cold. However, you have to treat your relationship with your child, custodial parent and court like a business deal. If you think about it, child support is money, contracts and agreements. When a father breaks that agreement, in many cases a forced agreement, most states hire and empower collection agencies to come after them. These collection agencies are like bouncers showing up at your door to collect a gambling debt for a gangster. If you don't have the money, your knees might be in danger of being bashed in.

It is very important to handle your situation in a professional and business-like manner. This means know what your child support agreement is. Then, do what it says. If you can't, communicate that to the collection agency.

Another part of handling your business is showing up to all court dates and hearings. I can't tell you how many times I've beat a traffic ticket by just showing up to traffic-court. Because the police officer, that issued me the ticket, didn't show up to court, I didn't have to say a word, and the judge just dismissed the ticket. However, when you don't show up for your court dates and hearings, most of the time, you will lose your case and things, such as contempt of court and warrants for your arrest will occur. I've been there and done all that! You don't want to go down that road.

Also, you might get lucky and win your case or get your child support amount lowered, simply, because the custodial parent didn't show up to court. Remember the child support system is really blind. So, keep this in mind and handle your business. Make every effort to appear at court hearings and respond appropriately to every letter you get in the mail concerning your case. In addition, show up for your scheduled visitations. If for whatever reason you can't, communicate that to the mother and child. Remember, bad things happen when you don't show up. So, by all means, SHOW UP!

TIP 7 **Play The Game Right**

Here is a quick overview on how to play the child support GAME!

> Step 1. Get A DNA Test
> Step 2. Become Legal
> Step 3. Get Visitation
> Step 4. Be Consistent

You Win!!!

This is the game plan, simplified. It is very important that you initiate all these steps, first. It will make you look more favorable to the judge. DNA tests will save you an appearance on "The Maury Povich Show." Becoming the legal father will give you equal rights. Visitation is with your child and is priceless. If anyone tries to interfere, you can press charges or gain full custody of the child. Being consistent with your visitations and commitments will make you look like "Superman" in your child's eyes. Now, these 4 steps will not be easy or cheap. However, it will be well worth all the money and trouble. So, follow the steps and win your game.

TIP 8 Keep Those Receipts

This is a habit you should practice even if things are going good in your relationship. No one can predict the future. Make notes and keep receipts on all your child's expenses. This may help you in the future. Also, keeping all of your receipts will be a help to clear up any future disputes on your income, if things go south one day. Chances are higher for you paying a lot more in child support if you don't have records of proof. So, keep track of all of your child's expenses, now! If conditions or your income changes, it will be easier to prove.

TIP 9 Keep The Peace

Keeping the peace might be a hard thing to do when emotions, egos, money and children are involved. However, I understand. I've been there, done that and bought the t-shirt. What I learned is that being on speaking terms is better than not being on speaking terms. Keeping lines of communication open with your ex is less likely to turn her into a financial monster. Don't argue or discuss money issues. Remember to handle your business. Your verbal comments or angry text messages may come back and bite you in the behind, later. If your ex wants to talk or argue about money concerns, tell her to voice any financial concerns with her child support caseworker. It seems cold. Unfortunately, you have to cover your end. I found out the hard way how trying to be nice and discussing finances with my ex could be used against me in court. In addition, I would give her hundreds of dollars, for some emergency, and the money would not be counted towards child support. I was told it was just a gift. If I just had paid extra on my child support payment, it would have been better for me. Now, I know there will be times when you have to take a loss for your child.

However, all financial transactions with your ex should be done with your child support agency. This will keep the peace.

TIP 10 Take Advantage Of Video And Audio

If you ever watch "Judge TV" shows, you will see more and more people bringing into court text messages, emails and facebook posts, as evidence against someone else. Be careful of comments and angry text messages. They can come back to hunt you.

I read a story, online, about a father who wore a wire while he was in contact with his ex-wife. During the meeting, there were some verbally abusive and angry threats made towards him. His attorney used a transcript from the tape and made a successful demonstration how hostile and uncaring his ex was towards him and his child. The judge was not impressed with his tactics. The judge felt it was just a way to bait the other person into losing their temper. I think using your smartphone, to tape conversations with your ex, is a good way to dismiss any false accusations or disputes against you. I believe this will only help you. Also, it will help in keeping the piece. Your ex will have a more polite tone if she knows she's being taped. Now, there's a chance the courts won't accept the tape or even listen. I say it's better to have them, just in case.

TIP 11 A Lawyer Can Make Or Break You

My experience with lawyers hasn't been pleasant. I almost would like to say that all lawyers are bad. However, I can't because I did have one that I felt really cared. He gave me great advice as well as represented me in court. He told the judge I was broke and that he was representing me, for free, as a favor for a family member. In addition, he got me out of the mess I was in at the same time. Later, he gave me his card and was gone. So, because of that, I felt he was an angel that really saved me. A few months later, I tried to call him to pay him, however, his number was invalid and he had moved out of his office. I think he really was an angel. Now, that was the Good, which was a rare exception. The next couple of times I dealt with lawyers, I experienced the Bad and the Ugly.

The Bad lawyer was one I retained after getting advice from someone I knew. They told me he was good and that he, also, was a judge. So, I finally thought I could get my child support problems in order. This lawyer asked for all of the child support paperwork I had from over the years. I gave him everything he asked for, as well as a check for

$250 to get started. In a lawyer's world, this was a steal of a deal. He told me he would meet me at the hearing. At the hearing, I noticed he seemed to be a little scattered. He was also chain-smoking. Every five minutes, he was going out side for a smoke. This man did absolutely nothing at the hearing. He was just there. After the hearing, he said we would be going to court. Then, he asked for another $250. Okay, I'll cut to the chase, here. Over the next couple of weeks, we met for hearings and he did the same thing. And, just like the other times, I would pay him $250. When we finally got in the courtroom, I was hoping my lawyer would be like the lawyers on television. You know, the ones who are always making a compelling argument about the case! I wanted him to let the judge know I was a good guy and that I loved my children. I wanted him to put my ex on the stand and leave her babbling. However, that's not what I got. What I got was a chain-smoking lawyer, with no backbone. He didn't argue a thing! He just stated I should give them whatever they ask for. Now, I decided to fight. However, because I went into the courtroom with a chain- smoking, only concerned about getting paid lawyer, the end result was the same as my lawyer, bad.

The next lawyer is what I call the Ugly. It makes me shiver to think what would have happen if this sorry excuse for a lawyer had been working for me. I think it would have definitely gotten ugly.

The very last time I was summoned to court, for an adjustment in the payments to child support, I was asked to do a deposition. In addition, I had to submit, once again, all of my financial records from the last 3 years. In the past, I would give the lawyers all of my paperwork; all neat and sorted by year and date. I made it easy for them to cut my throat. This time, I put all the files, for each year, in it's own box. It was, somewhat, sorted; but, it would take work on their part to sort everything out. I handed the boxes of paperwork over to the lawyer that was representing my ex. After handing it over to him, he looked surprised that I had everything they had asked for. He also saw there were hundreds, if not thousands of receipts, back statements, payroll checkstubs and an assortment of financial documents.

He put the boxes on the long brown table, which had at least twelve black leather chairs parked neatly and equally spaced beneath it. He then lifted one of the lids off the boxes and fumbled through the contents with fake concern. He closed the lid and asked me a few important questions. I realized, then, that he was using the deposition as a weapon to scare me. I also realized he could care less about the contents of the three huge boxes, before him. His tactic may have worked if he had tried that on me fifteen years earlier. However, it wasn't working now. He was lazy. He could have held me up to three hours. They asked could they keep my paperwork. I said I wasn't comfortable with that. They held me there for only an hour.

This lawyer's behavior continued right on into court. Before we could go in front of a judge, we had to go into mediation. They wanted more money and I said I couldn't pay more. As a matter of fact, I asked for a reduction. The lazy lawyer was very similar to the "Bad" lawyer I had. This time, I had no lawyer; but, I did my homework and knew what my rights were. I figured the lazy lawyer only cared about getting paid. I was pretty sure my ex paid him up front. So, I'm sure that made him even lazier. I almost felt bad for her, almost.

When we finally became face to face with the judge, my ex and her lawyer looked so unorganized and was asking for some ridiculous amount of money for a child that was eighteen years old. This lazy lawyer made her look greedy. However, he made me look like a saint, even though, at this particular time, I wasn't able to pay the court ordered $1,200 a month child support payments. I had been making consistent payments of about $100 a week. This was the amount being garnished from a part-time job. I had been paying what I could for about two years. Remember Commandment # 7? It stated "Thou Shall ~ Pay Something." The very last time I was in court, for child support, I won. The judge reduced my payment of $1,200 a month to $400 a month. That was the last time I was ever in court for child support, and it ended on a happy note for me.

TIP 12 **Never Stop Handling Your Business**

Believe it or not, I got kind of relaxed at the end of my dealings with the child support system. I knew I had to be close to the end of what I owed. Keep in mind that at this point, my kids were all grown; twenty-seven and twenty-four years old. I owed about $13,000 to their mother and $7,500 to the state of Florida for all the welfare or state assistance the mother received over the years. I was ordered to pay $400 a month until everything was paid off. I had a part-time job that I worked for five years. The check that was garnished took care of about 90% of all the debt. The other 10% was paid for by my income tax that was taken. Now, with all that being said, I felt I had to be really close to being finished paying. As I said, I slacked off sending in my payments on time. In addition, I had dropped down to sending just $100 a month. Well, slacking off, missing payments as well as sending in partial payments equaled a BIG MISTAKE! I soon received a familiar letter in the mail that I hadn't seen for at least seven years. It was a notice that my driver's license would be suspended if I didn't catch up on my child support payments. I had about one month to do so. What was even more disturbing was the letter stated that I owed $6,500 in arrears, still. I was stunned at that amount. I knew that amount was off. This is when I stopped slacking off and started handling my business. The first thing I did was called the office to find out when I could come down and do a face to face with a caseworker. They offered to discuss it with me over the phone. However, I refused. Secondly, I prepared for the meeting. I gathered all my check stubs as well as any related paperwork for my case. Third, I went in for my appointment, which was quite an ordeal. I had to mentally prepare for a long day, in a building, with major tension coming from everyone that entered. The tension was so thick you could cut it with a knife.

The child support office kind of reminded me of a dirty greyhound station. It had dark floors that seemed to be, somewhat, sticky. There were confused people wandering in a long line waiting to speak to someone behind what resembled a bulletproof glass.

After a three hour wait to speak to a child support representative, I negotiated reduced payments in order to stop my driver's license from being suspended. They needed 10% of the total owed, which was $650. I got them down to $600 and gave them half. The other half would be due in thirty days, along with the regular child support payment of $200. I was also told that I no longer owed the mother arrears. However, I still owed $200 to the state of Florida. In case you haven't been keeping up with how much I needed to pay in order to keep my driver's license, it totaled one thousand dollars. As you can see, this was getting very confusing and expensive. The last thing I did was to ask for a complete audit of my case. The audit came about due to me slacking off in regards to my payments. About two months later, I received a letter I had been waiting to receive for over twenty-five years. This was the letter I thought would never come. It stated that my child support case had been closed and all my debt was paid.

Guys, I can't even begin to explain what it felt like to get that letter. I hope that any man, who's on child support, get to experience that feeling.

TIP 13 Even During Good Times, Protect Yourself

A lot of men make the mistake of not handling their business during good times. Good times means both you and the mother are still in a relationship. Unfortunately, this too often becomes a Pearl Harbor type of situation. I've seen time and time again men devastated when their loving girlfriend transforms into an evil beast. There is a real reason for the old saying, "There is no wrath like a woman scorned." So, my advice is never stop handling your business. Think of handling your business like a prenuptial agreement. This prenuptial will put you in a better position for your child if for any reason you and your girlfriend should ever end the relationship. For example, a friend of mine and his girlfriend were in a shaky relationship. The two were constantly breaking up and getting back together. At a certain point, she put him on child support. No surprise to me, they got back together; however, she didn't close the child support case. They started living together and he ignored the child support case, for years. He figured that since he was living with his girlfriend and child as well as paying most of the bills, the child support would no longer be an issue. He couldn't be more wrong! Later on, after breaking up, he discovered he owed over $27,000 in back child support and penalties. He tried to get it reduce, but the judge wouldn't hear it. In addition, the girlfriend said he hadn't given her money in years. So, he had to pay.

So, again, HANDLE YOUR BUSINESS!

TIP 14 **Know That Money Isn't Real**

There is one last thought that I want you to have an open mind to. I want you to wrap your mind around the fact that money isn't real. I know that it's a mind-blowing concept, especially in today's world. However, it isn't real. It is an illusion. I feel it was created for one purpose: to control people or make them do what other people want. I guess you can look at it like doggy treats. The original concept was based on the gold standard; meaning for every dollar printed, there was a dollar worth of gold in some bank vault to make it valuable. Now, that seemed like a good system, at first. However, I have a question. If the gold makes the dollar valuable, then what makes the gold valuable? The answer is simple. People like you and me make the gold valuable. It's what you will do for it. Like I said, it's a doggy treat. Just think about some of the things people will do. People will lie, steal and even kill for it. What are you willing to do for it? Are you willing to abandon your children because child support wants your doggy treats? Will you beat or hurt your ex-wife, girlfriend or lover because she placed you on child support? Is spending quality time with your child or children less important than the doggy treats you're having to give up? I think you get my point. Please don't get caught up in the matrix or the illusion of money! The only thing that is real is your child or children's love, period! Keep that your focus and LOVE them, instead.

MY RUNNING STORY:
26 Year Journey Ending On Broadway

Forest Gump was one of my favorite movies. One thing that stood out in the Forest Gump movie was the white feather that would appear in different scenes. That feather would float through the wind, aimlessly; but, somehow, it all tied together.

The year was 2012. I was in a small theater on Broadway, in New York City. After being handed a program, I was shown to my seat. Though the seats were narrow, I was thankful just to have a seat since the theater was sold out. This was opening night of my daughter's first Broadway play. It was so exciting! I immediately took notice of the media, the lights as well as the cameras flashing. I began to reminisce on how different this was compared to how the story began, 28 years ago.

It began with two teenagers. One was 16 years old and the other was 17 years old; sitting in a child support office. The 16-year-old girl was nine months pregnant at the time and the 17-year old boy was signing child support papers so that the 16-year-old girl could receive public assistance. Realizing where the journey had started and where the journey was finally ending, with my daughter's Broadway debut, it was all worth it.

Blah Blah Blah
"INCARCERATION"
Blah Blah Blah…

I didn't just decide to stop running on my own accord. I was summoned to a hearing about my massive arrearage, which had amounted up to well over $14,000. I figured it would be the same ole conversation. I had been to hearings several times before and I'd do the same song and dance. They'd ask me for money and I'd tell them I didn't have any. However, this time, it was different. When I finally was asked to step into the room, where the hearing was being held, I noticed that everyone looked stiff and very official. It was in what seemed to be a meeting room, instead of a courtroom. So, I relaxed and just went with the flow. Well, in between all of their blah blah blah, they stopped and said something had to be signed, or something about the paperwork was wrong and missing. They wanted to postpone the hearing out a few weeks, unless I wanted to move forward. Everyone got quiet in the room and looked at me as if I was E.F. Hutton. Now, that was my first warning that something was wrong. After all my past dealings with child support, I should have recognized something wasn't right. I should have just said I wanted to postpone. But, I was relaxed and I felt "what the heck." What's the worst that can happen? After all, the hearing was in a meeting room. So, I said, "I'd like to move forward." I don't know what I was thinking! Well, they proceeded and I just set back in my chair, just wanting it to be over. I wasn't really listening to all of the "thee's and thou's." But, then I kind of heard the word "Incarceration," "blah, blah, blah," "60 days," "blah, blah." Then, I heard the slamming of the gavel. BAM! At that point, I was sitting up in my chair. A big police officer walked over and lightly tapped me on my shoulder and whispered for me to step into another room with him. I still wasn't quite sure what was happening. But, I figured it was over and they needed more information from me. I could not have been more wrong. As soon as I stepped in the next room and the door closed, I was asked to turn around and place my hands behind my back and was promptly arrested. I was sentenced to pay $1,000 or spend 60 days in jail. From that point on, child support had my undivided attention and I taught myself how to play the game.

6 A.M...Police At My Door

I had finally started getting things together. After years of working as a bellman, I went to school and got a degree in graphic design. I moved to Atlanta, Georgia, got married and established a successful graphic design company. I managed to land two big contracts; one with Home Depot and another with So So Def Recordings. I also partnered with some friends in Florida and started a school-touring company. My wife and I sold our house and found a bigger house where we moved to in January '2003. Things were going GREAT! That is, until I got a 6 a.m. knock at my door! It seems like that knock started a swift fall from grace, at the time. It came from the hand of a sheriff that was serving me a court summons to appear in court. I was totally shocked! I was, somewhat, current on my payments. So, I couldn't imagine why I would have to go to court, again. Of course, I went to see what they wanted from me. My children's mother had heard about all my recent success and decided to exercise her right in asking for a substantial increase in child support. She wanted an increase from $496 a month to $800 a month. I was pissed! That was more than I was paying for my mortgage, at the time. I decided I was going to fight her in court. I found a lawyer and started the process. It took about year. Nevertheless, that 6 a.m. knock started a downward financial spiral, for me. As they say, "when it rains, it pours." First, the contract with Home Depot ended. I had been there for a year and a half. So So Def Recordings started a slow downsizing, after the owner began experiencing tax problems. My hours, there, had been reduced to part-time. The school-touring business was grossing a lot of money. However, it wasn't coming my way because I only held one-fourth ownership of the company. In addition, it was based out of Florida, and my job was only to find the talent and handle the graphics and advertising. Reflecting back on it, now, what was I thinking? The school-touring company had appointed me treasurer of the company. Yet, I wasn't a signer on the company's bank account. I didn't even see any of the money that was coming and going. Still, on paper, it looked like I was part owner of a company that had grossed $350,000 for the year.

Lift Up Your Head

I wasn't prepared for the lawyers of the other team playing dirty, in court. Before we even got started, my lawyer suggested that I should settle the case before we go in front of the judge. I said okay. We can try. But, I knew their mother, and it wasn't about money. It was about blood! She was using the courts to seek revenge because of all the pain she felt I caused her over the years. We offered an increase of child support to $650 a month, for one child. You see, my daughter was eighteen, had just graduated from high school and was all grown up. For years, I had been paying $496 a month, for two. So, I felt offering $650, for one, was a fair offer. They rejected my offer and countered it with $800 a month. I felt that $800 was outrageous! So, I said, okay, we'll take it to the judge. Once again, what was I thinking? Her lawyer started painting a financial masterpiece in front of the judge. The judge subpoenaed my CPA and all my financial records, 3 years back. Bank statements, savings accounts, checking accounts and even my current wife's information were offered to the judge. At one point, I felt like a mob boss. It seemed like the whole courtroom was occupied with my case.

In addition to myself were my CPA, my lawyer, his two assistants, my children's mother, her husband, the judge, court reporters and several police officers. All just for my case!

Lets get back to the financial picture the lawyer had started to paint for the judge. He began his argument to the judge with "Your Honor, Mr. Patterson wants you to believe that he is only making $36,000, a year. However, we have proof that Mr. Patterson has been making around, at least, $500,000, this year alone." From there, he started presenting what I like to call "fuzzy" math. Under his calculations, he could make one hundred dollars look like two hundred dollars. This is how he did it. I had three bank accounts: personal checking, business checking and a personal savings account. Okay, if I got paid one hundred dollars from a client, I would deposit it into my business account. I would, then, write an eighty dollar check from my business account to my personal account. I'd leave 20% in the business account for taxes. Then, I would take twenty dollars from my personal checking account and put it in my savings account. Under his "fuzzy" math, I'd made $200 in deposits. But, I didn't. I had only dispersed the $100 to other bank accounts.

Now, imagine applying it to thousands of dollars and checks. He made it look like I had over one hundred thousand dollars, plus, I was treasurer of my school-touring company, which had grossed over $350,000 that year. I was also working for a multi-million dollar record company, So So Def Recordings.

By the time he finished, the judge and I were confused. My lawyer was terrible! He was just there to get a check. He didn't, at all, present or argue my case. Yes, I was around a lot of money. However, gross and net are two, totally, different things. My bank statements were correct. I had only made $36,000 that year. The years before, I had made $65,000. But, I had lost a major contract. In addition, I was part-time at the record label. If my lawyer would have conveyed that to the judge, I think I would have had a better day in court.

After hearing both sides, the judge made her ruling. The judge said to me, "Mr. Patterson, I'm a little confused about how much money you, actually, make. However, I have at my discretion the ability to make a ruling on an assumption." She continued on, "Mr. Patterson, you are very talented. You have your own company, and you work for a major record label. Now, I'm not sure what you're making; but, I believe if you tried real hard, you could make $60,000 a year. So I'm making my ruling that you are to pay $1,000 a month plus $200 for arrears, for a total amount of $1,200 a month."

The judge's words were like a knife in my heart. It hurt so bad! All I could do was lay my head down on the table. Then, one of the cops walked over and tapped me on my shoulder and said, "Lift up your head, please."

A Lot Of Money, And No Pay

That court ruling, basically, wiped out my part of the income in my marriage. One of the hardest things I had ever had to do was to have to come home and tell my wife that we had lost the fight in court. Not only did we lose, I had to pay more than they had originally asked for. To compound the problem, we were supposed to purchase a new home that my wife had fallen in love with. After giving her that news, I hugged her and reassured her that someway, somehow, we would be alright. Then she said, "I'll call the realtor and let her know we will not be moving forward in buying our new home." I told my wife she was not doing that. I refused to let my past stop my future. I would just have to work harder than I had ever had in my life. I was determined to move forward. Life went on; and, for about a year, I was able to make my child support payments. I stepped up my hustle. I was still working for the record label and also doing freelance graphics. I wasn't getting a lot of freelance work. However, it was just enough to cover my child support. I had to do some creative financing; and, I was making it until the bottom fell out, again.

It was 2003 and it seemed that the economy had hit rock bottom. By 2004, I was unemployed and wasn't able to find freelance graphic work. I searched and searched for jobs.

But, I couldn't find anything long-term. In the meantime, I had a bigger problem lurking. You see, I had that twelve hundred dollar child support payment that I was not in a position to pay. I was falling behind, fast. It seemed like a doomed situation. What I didn't know was that my luck was about to change. The strangest thing occurred. My lucky break came from Child Support Services.

Shelter From The Storm

One day, I received a letter in the mail from child support services. The letter asked me to enter a program called "Fatherhood." This program was for fathers who had been trying to do the right thing and paying their child support; but, for some reason, they had fallen behind in their payments. It could have been due to the loss of a job, health issues, family issues, or other personal reasons. Also, you could not just join the "Fatherhood" program. You had to be referred by a child support caseworker. Once you were placed in the program, you would receive shelter from the storm of penalties that normally happens when a man falls behind on his child support payments. The normal penalties were things like a driver's license suspension, business license suspension, wage garnishment or being arrested. As a part of being in the program, you had to attend weekly meetings. If you missed the meetings, you would be kicked out of the program. The meetings reminded me of an AAA meeting. It was a bunch of guys in a room with the same look on their faces. The look of "How did we end up here?" I really thought like most of the other guys, in the room, that this would be a waste of time. I couldn't have been more wrong. As a matter of fact, those meetings inspired me to write this book. It turned out that the "Fatherhood" program wasn't really a part of the child support system. It was a non-profit organization. Its instructor/founder was a rebel and an advocate for men in the child support system. He began to school all of the men in the class on the system and how to use it to our advantage. So, I thought I'd take what I learned in that program and what I've learned over 25 years, in the child support system, and put it in the pages of a book. I want you to know that there is light at the end of the tunnel, and you can make it. If I can make it through the system, anyone can.

Eyes Wide Open

I found the "Fatherhood" program to be very interesting. One of the first things I learned is that I wasn't alone. The program was taught in like a high school setting, with the teacher in front of about fifteen desks. In those desks were men from all walks of life. In other words, there were blacks, whites, latinos and middle eastern. It didn't matter if you were middle-class or poor. Everyone had one thing in common. We were all victims of the system. In every word this man spoke, it was like pulling open a curtain that had been veiling my eyes for 18 years. He began to tell us we had rights. Up until that point, I felt like we didn't have any rights, at all; only the name "Deadbeat Dads." It was during this time that I found out that the child support system wasn't personal, just flawed. Now, mix that with politics and you have a real mess on your hands. Child support is a subject most politicians and/or public figures won't touch with a ten-foot pole.

BEST FEELING IN THE WORLD

Owing Nothing And No One

I have to be honest. I fought the process with tooth and nails the whole way. But, now at the end of the child support process, I realized it all worked out for my good. It's like that quote from the Bible that reads "You meant it for evil but God meant it for good." That is how I feel about the child support system. Some mean it for evil and there are others who mean it for good. I say that because there is no greater feeling, as a man, to say to the world, no one had to pay for my children. I have to say it is a very good feeling!

Now, I'm not saying that it wasn't challenging dealing with the children's mother, child support workers, lawyers and judges. However, I survived it all. If I can make it through this broken child support system, I know you can as well. Please don't give up hope. If you've been knocked down by the child support system, get up, dust yourself off and use this book to turn it around. It may not be easy… but nothing good ever is. You're fighting for your child. There's nothing more important than that. NEVER GIVE UP!!!

THE SOLUTION
A New Idea

I have had a long relationship with the child support system. I've spent many years witnessing its many flaws. Many people are aware of those flaws. I hear men complaining all the time. It seems no one has a solution. Well, here is an idea that maybe a part of the final solution. I believe if there was a universal child support cap as well as some type of future support, depending on your tax bracket, the maximum you would pay on one child per month would be twenty-five thousand dollars. With this idea, it wouldn't matter if you were a millionaire, etc. Currently, in the state of Georgia, your child support for one child is around 20% of your gross income each month. So, to give a simple example: If you made one thousand dollars a month, your child support would be set at two hundred dollars per month. Now, this sounds fair until you get into bigger numbers. Say you make $200,000 each month. That means that you would have to pay forty thousand dollars a month, for one child. I don't think that is fair to the child or the father. It's not fair to the child because that child would never get 98% of that money. And it's not fair to the father because he knows that child can't eat $40,000 worth of food or even buy that much in clothes every month.

Most fathers know the majority of the forty thousand will be spent by the mother buying cars, hair, nails, clothes, vacations, jewelry, etc. Remember, that money isn't for the mother. It's called child support. Now, under my current and future child support plan, using those same numbers of the father making $200,000 a month, he would still have to pay the same 20% of his gross income for his one child. The difference is the money would be split. $20,000 would go to the child's current needs each month. The other $20,000 would go into a trust fund for the child's future needs and the child will only be able to withdraw the money at the age of 25. The child can decide to give to his or her mother, that's fine. I feel this plan kills two birds with one stone. First, it stops the mother from using their kids as lotto tickets. Secondly, it may ensure the mother treats the child the with the love and warmth expected if she wants to get any of that child's money, once that child turns twenty-five.

WHAT NOW?
Do something powerful and positive. Buy a book for a friend, your son, someone else's son or a male student.
In addition, tell every guy you know to read this book.
You just might be helpful in someone's life.

TOGETHER WE CAN CHANGE
THE CHILD SUPPORT SYSTEM

TELL US YOUR STORY.

We'd like to know if any of the Ten Commandments or Tips
was helpful to you. Let us hear your story,
as well as any helpful advice you'd like to share.
Your story or advice could be included in a future book.
Email: sirrod@dontbully.org
www.dontbully.org

Dont Bully, Inc.
836 Flat Shoals Rd SE
Suite C #239
Conyers, GA 30094

VOCABULARY

A ─────────────────

Access - Parenting Time (once called Visitation)

Acquit - To find a criminal defendant not guilty

Action - A dispute taken to court to be settled; same as "case," "suit" and "lawsuit" when used in the courtroom context

Adjudicate - To make a final decision; to give a judgment or a decree

Administrative Process - A quasi-judicial system created by statute or rule to determine legal rights

Admissible - Evidence that is properly introduced in a trial

Adversary System - Method used in the courts of the United States to settle legal disputes. Both parties in the case tell their story to the judge and/or jury for resolution

Affiant - Someone who makes and signs an affidavit

Affidavit - A written statement of fact, signed and sworn to in front of a notary or a person who has the right to administer an oath

Affirm - To uphold a decision made by a lower court. Age of Majority -Age at which the duty of support terminates (Currently age 18 in most States unless the child is actually attending high school, a certified high school equivalency program, or is disabled) Aid to Families with Dependent Children

(AFDC) - A category of public assistance paid on behalf of children who are deprived of support by one or both of their parents due to disability, or continued absence (including desertion) from the home

Alimony - See Spousal Maintenance in this Glossary

Allegations - Statements against one party, which the other party is prepared to prove

Alleged Father (Putative Father) - A person who has been named as the father of a child born out of wedlock, but for whom paternity has not yet been established

Alternative Dispute Resolution (ADR) - A process to resolve a dispute in lieu of traditional litigation; e.g. mediation, arbitration or settlement conferences

Answer - Written response in a civil case; in it the defendant admits or denies the allegations of the plaintiff's complaint and states any defenses that apply

Appeal - A request made to a higher court to reverse or modify a decision made by a lower court

Appearance - By coming into court, a defendant agrees to abide by the jurisdiction of the court; gives to the court an address to which the court can mail notices of hearings and other court documents; and a document identifying someone who is representing another. An attorney files a Notice of Appearance, making it known to the court that she or he is representing a specific individual

Appellant - The person/party appealing the judgment or decision of a court

Appellate Court - A court having jurisdiction (authority) to hear appeals

Appellee - The party against whom the appeal is taken

Applicant/Recipient (AR) - One who applies for and receives AFDC, Medical Assistance or Food Stamp benefits or any other type of public assistance

Arbitration - Binding Voluntary Arbitration: A process in which the disputing parties choose a neutral person to hear their dispute and resolve it by rendering a final and binding decision or award. Arbitration is an adversarial, adjudicative process designed to resolve the specific issues submitted by the parties. Arbitration differs significantly from litigation in that (1) it does not require conformity with the legal rules of evidence and procedure, (2) there is flexibility in timing and choice of decision makers and (3) the proceeding is conducted in private rather than in a public forum. Binding arbitration awards are usually enforceable by courts, absent defects in the arbitration procedures. Mandatory Non-binding Arbitration: Describes court-annexed arbitration programs. Court-appointed arbitrators hear cases subject to jurisdictional limits set by each county. The losing party has the right to a trial de novo (new trial) in the trial court

Arbitrator - An attorney selected to hear a case and settle the legal dispute without a formal trial

Arraignment - Court proceeding in which the defendant stands before the judge to answer criminal charges by entering a plea of guilty or not guilty

Arrearage/Arrears - An amount of money that is overdue; usually this refers to the amount of child support that has been ordered but has not been paid on time

Arrearage/Arrears Judgment - a written judicial determination of the amount of support past due for a specific period of time

Assignment of Rights - An eligibility requirement for TANF whereby the applicant/recipient must assign to the state all rights to support he or she may have in their own behalf or on behalf of a dependent child

Assistant Judge - See Judge in this Glossary

Attachment - The act of seizing a person or property under the authority of a judicial order so that the person or property is before the court, subject to its judgment

Attorney-at-Law - One who is admitted to the State Bar of

State and who may represent clients in legal proceedings; also called lawyers or counselors

B

Bail - Money or other form of security the judge requires to be held by the court to ensure that a criminal defendant, released while awaiting trial, will be in court for the trial. Bail is returned when the defendant returns for trial

Bailiff - Courtroom attendant responsible for keeping order in the courtroom and supervising the jury

Bench -The seat where a judge sits in court

Biological Father - The man who fathers a child by impregnating the mother

Board of Supervisors - Local governing body at the county level Brief - Written statement explaining facts of a case and laws that apply

Burden of Proof - The obligation placed on one of the parties in a dispute to prove their allegations in order to obtain relief from the court

C

Caretaker Relative - A person who receives TANF payments on behalf of a beneficiary incapable of managing the funds

Case - Lawsuit, suit or action being resolved through the court system

Case Law - Law composed of previous written decisions of appellate courts

Case Number - A number assigned by the court to identify your specific case; the case number in domestic relations is usually preceded by one or two letters such as D, DO, or DR

Central Registry - An entity required by all reciprocating jurisdictions to receive, log and distribute interstate cases

Certified Copy - A copy of a paper, which has been signed and certified as a true copy by the officer in whose custody the original is entrusted

Chambers - Private offices of a judge or justice; Chief Justice, Presiding justice of the Supreme Court

Child Support - An amount of money that a parent must pay to another parent to contribute to the living, medical and educational expenses of a child

Child Support Enforcement Administration (CSEA) - See Division of Child Support Enforcement (DCSE)

Child Support Guidelines - Standards adopted by the State Supreme Court to guide parents and the courts when determining child support obligations

Child Support Order - A written order from the court that states which parent must pay child support; which parent will receive child support; the amount of child support payment; how often the payment must be made

Child Support Worksheet - A document, used to enter financial information and calculate the amount of child support according to the Child Support Guidelines

Civil Action or Suit - A non-criminal case concerning the claim of one individual or entity against another

Civil Law - Area of law that deals with disputes between individuals, not involving crimes

Claim - Legal and factual grounds for a court to grant relief Clearinghouse - A central location that receives, disburses and monitors IV-D support payments

Clerk of the Court - An appointed or elected official who is responsible for keeping records and accounts for a court and managing routine affairs Code of Federal Regulations (CFR) - Rules implementing federal laws. In IV-D, these rules are contained in 45 CFR Part 300-399

Complaint - Legal paper telling the court and the defendant what the plaintiff's claims are. This document is filed with the court at the beginning of a case

Conciliation Court - A branch of the Superior Court to which a spouse may apply in an effort to preserve a marriage or from whom a parent may request assistance in settling disputes regarding children

Conclusions of Law - The decision made by the judge by applying the law to the facts of the case

Constable - An elected official whose primary duty is to deliver and return legal notices and documents as directed by a Justice of the Peace

Contempt - A willful disregard or disobedience of the court's order

Contested Case - An action in which the defendant opposes the relief sought by the plaintiff

Continuance - Postponement of a court hearing **Contract** - An agreement that may be enforceable through a court action

Conviction - A decision by the judge or a verdict by the jury determining that a person charged with a criminal offense is guilty beyond a reasonable doubt

Counsel - See Lawyer or Attorney at Law in this Glossary

Counterclaim - A claim asserted by a defendant against the plaintiff

County Attorney - Attorney elected in each county to prosecute criminal cases on behalf of the public and to represent the county in civil matters

Court Administrator - Person who assists the presiding judge in managing the court

Court Commissioner - Person with authority to do the job of a judge in certain types of cases

Court of Record - Courts in which a record is made of all proceedings. Justice of the Peace and Municipal Courts are not courts of record, but they sometimes do keep records of court proceedings

Court Reporter - A person who records courtroom proceedings in order to be able to produce a transcript of the proceeding

Courtroom Clerk - Person in charge of making and keeping the docket of court proceedings and other court records

Crime - An act forbidden by law and punishable by fine, probation, imprisonment or death Custodial Parent/Person, (CP) The parent (or parents, in joint custody situations) designated by the court to make major decisions regarding a child's care

Custody - See Parental Rights and Responsibilities in this Glossary

D

Decree - The court's final decision on a case brought before it

Default - A failure of the defendant to file the appropriate papers within the time allowed or to appear in court during a scheduled hearing

Default Judgment - Relief granted by a court when an opposing party fails to answer a complaint or appear for trial

Defendant - The person against whom a lawsuit is started; sometimes this person is called a respondent

Delinquent Act - An act committed by a juvenile that if committed by an adult would be a crime

Denial - An answer to a complaint in which the defendant denies the allegations made by the plaintiff

Department of Economic Security (DES) - The agency in State responsible for overseeing the IV-D and public assistance programs and to coordinate their activities

Department of Health and Human Services (DHHS) - Federal agency which includes the Office of Child Support Enforcement (OCSE)

Dependency - A relationship in which one depends on another for support in whole or in part

Deponent - Someone who gives a deposition

Deposition - Testimony taken orally or in writing outside of a courtroom by question and answer under oath. It may be read in court and may be admitted by the judge as evidence

Discovery - The procedures available to a party to a lawsuit to learn relevant facts which are known to other parties or witnesses, in order to enable the party to prepare for trial

Dismiss - To close out a case without granting the relief sought in the complaint; a case may be dismissed by the parties or by the court

Disregard - In TANF cases, the amount of child support, up to $50, actually paid by the obligor and disbursed to the aid recipient in addition to the monthly TANF grant. Termed "disregard" because it is not considered by IV-A to determine TANF eligibility

Dissolution of Marriage - The term used in State Law for "divorce"

Division of Child Support Enforcement (DCSE) - The division of DES charged with the statewide administration and operation of IV-D child support programs

DNA Testing - A way to determine the parents of a child by testing the chromosomes of each parent and child through taking a blood sample

Docket - A written list containing brief notes of all the important acts done in court in each case. The name " docket" or " trial docket" is sometimes given to the list or calendar of cases set for trial or other hearings at a specified time and date

Docket Number - A number that is given to each case as it is filed in the court. This number should be listed on all papers that are filed with the court

Domestic Relations - Branch of the law that deals with families and children

Duty of Support - The legal obligations of each parent to support minor natural or adopted un-emancipated child. In State this obligation continues past the age of majority (currently age 18) if the child is still attending high school or in a certified high school equivalency program, or when the child as minor was found to be disabled and the court has ordered the payments to continue

E

Emancipation - A status of independence of children from their parents due to age or circumstance

Evidence - Testimony of a witness, an object or written documents submitted in court regarding the facts in a case

Excess - The remaining amount of a support payment forwarded to the TANF family in addition to the $50 disregard after the state has retained a portion to reimburse itself for the current month's TANF grant. The excess plus the $50 disregard will not, however, exceed the amount of the current support set out in the court order

Exhibit - A document or object that is offered into evidence during a trial or hearing

Ex Parte - Latin phrase for relief that is sought (and may be granted) without notice to the opposing party; commonly used in obtaining an order of protection

Execution - A legal remedy used to enforce a judgment, by which a law enforcement officer may confiscate property of the debtor. Also refers to the process of serving a civil arrest warrant

F

Family Court - A trial court that has jurisdiction over all family cases; including divorce, child support, parentage, domestic abuse and juvenile cases

Family Law Commissioner - A judicial officer appointed in the superior court to establish and enforce support orders in IV-D cases

Federal Parent Locator Service (FPLS) - A national system operated by OCSE for the purpose of searching federal government records to locate parents

Felony - A serious crime, punishable by imprisonment in a state penitentiary. In some cases, the death penalty can be imposed

Filing Fee - Amount of money charged by the court when a case is started

Findings or Findings of Fact - Rulings by a court as to what facts are true

Forcible Entry and Detainer - A special proceeding for returning possession of lands, tenements or other real property to a person who has been wrongfully kept off the land or deprived of use of the land. This is a common proceeding used in landlord/tenant disputes, also known as eviction

Full Faith & Credit - The constitutional principle, which entitles a judgment of one state's court to recognition and enforcement in any other state's court

G

Garnishee - The person upon whom a garnishment is served; (Verb: to institute garnishment proceedings)

Garnishment - A legal remedy whereby a debtor's property or money in the possession or under the control of a third person (garnishee) is withheld from the debtor and applied to the debt

General Jurisdiction Court (Superior Court) - Court that has authority to hear all legal actions not assigned exclusively to another court

Genetic Testing - A way to determine the parents of a child by testing the chromosomes of each parent and child through taking a blood sample

Grand Jury - A group of 12-16 citizens who usually serve a term of not more than 120 days to hear or investigate charges of criminal behavior. TA Grand Jury indictment is a written accusation charging a defendant with commission of a crime

Grantee Relative - A relative who has physical or legal custody of and is receiving public assistance for another person's child

Guardian - A person appointed by the court to manage the affairs of a child or incapacitated person. Note: A guardian does not have a duty of support to the child in his/her care

Guardian Ad Litem - A person appointed by the court to represent the interests of a minor child in a divorce or parentage case. Guardian ad litem are different from attorneys in that they make a recommendation to the court about what they think is best for the child. Attorneys must tell the court what their clients (including children) want even if it is not in their best interests

H

Hearing - A proceeding scheduled by the court at a particular date and time that may include presentation of evidence by the parties

Home Study - A professional investigation of the living situation of each of the parents for the court's use in determining parental rights and responsibilities; also done to investigate persons seeking to adopt a child

I

Impeach - A formal accusation by the State House of Representatives that a public official committed misconduct in office Incorrigible - Refers to a juvenile who is unmanageable by parents or guardians. Incorrigible offenses include running away and truancy

Indictment - A formal, written accusation by a grand jury charging that a person or business committed a specific crime

In Forma Pauperis - Latin phrase referring to someone who does not have the financial ability to pay for all or part of the cost of litigation. A person may seek in forma pauperis status in order not to have to pay filing fees or the cost of serving papers on the other party. Sometimes this is abbreviated "IFP"

In Loco Parentis - Latin phrase referring to a person who, although not the legal or biological parent of the child, has been treated as a parent by the child and established a meaningful parental relationship over a substantial period of time

Initial Appearance - The first appearance by a party in a criminal case

Initiating Jurisdiction/State - A county, district or state in which a legal action is initiated; used most often in reference to interstate cases Injunction - An order of the court directing a person not to do certain things. For example an injunction in a dissolution case orders the spouses not to sell any of the community property Insolvency - Inability or lack of means to pay debts

Intercept - Seizure of a non-custodial parent's federal or state tax refund, or lottery winnings for application to a child support obligation

Interest on Support Arrearage - The annual rate of interest on support arrearages in State is 10% is currently the law

Interrogatories - Written questions of one party, which are served on the other party, who must answer by written replies under oath

Interstate - A case in which involves two or more states

Intrastate - A case in which involves two or more courts within a state

Irretrievably Broken - The standard used in State by the court to decide if a divorce should be granted. It means that there is no reasonable chance that the spouses will agree to stay married

IV-A - Title IV-A of the federal Social Security Act is that portion of the federal law covering the public assistance program

IV-A Referral - The notice (now automatically provided through computer interface) provided to IV-D by IV-A when an applicant/recipient is determined to be eligible for public assistance benefits IV-D - "Four D" refers to the title in the federal Social Security Act under which the Office of Child Support is reimbursed for providing service to persons who receive public assistance or who otherwise apply for their services

IV-D TANF Case - A case managed by the IV-D agency in which public assistance benefits are being paid for the child involved. Automatically referred to IV-D from IV-A when benefits paid

IV-D Agency - The entity responsible to administer the State Plan under Title IV-D of the Social Security Act

IV-D Non-TANF Case or Non-Public Assistance (NPA) - A case managed by the IV-D agency in which no public assistance benefits are being paid for the child involved (Application must be made in writing) IV-E - Title IV-E of the federal Social Security Act which provides for foster care maintenance payments for children who are IV-A eligible

J

Judge - One who presides over a given case on a given day

Judge Pro Tempore - A person assigned to perform the duties of a judge on a temporary basis

Judgment - The findings and order of the court, set forth in a formal written document signed by the judge

Judicial Performance Review - The process as required by the State Constitution to periodically review the performance of judges appointed by the governor

Jurisdiction - The power or authority of the court to act. The court must have jurisdiction over the subject matter or geographic area of the proceeding and the person against whom relief is sought

Jury Commissioner - Court officer who ensures that potential jurors are available to serve when needed by the courts

L

Law - Provisions which regulate the conduct of society, primarily generated by the legislative brand of government

Lawyer - A person licensed by the State to represent people in court and give legal advice

Legal Father - A man who is recognized by law as being a parent

Lien - A legal claim against another person's property as security for a debt

Limited Jurisdiction Court - A Court which may hear and decide limited types of case matters or limited financial sanctions. Examples of these are the Justice of the Peace and Municipal Courts

Litigant - A generic term used to describe a party to a legal action. A litigant can be a plaintiff or a defendant

Litigation - A judicial contest which seeks a decision from the court Long-Arm Statute - A statute permitting a state court to exercise jurisdiction over a non-resident

M

Magistrate - See Judge in this Glossary

Maintenance Supplement - An amount of money added to a child support award in order to ensure that the child lives in the same living conditions, as the child would have if the child had been living with the other parent. This amount is technically granted to one of the parents, and can be permanent or temporary

MAO - Medical Assistance Only cases Mediation - A process in which the disputing parties use a third party to assist them in reaching a settlement of the dispute. The process is private, informal, and non-binding. The mediator has no power to impose a settlement, but rather attempts to assist the disputants in reaching a mutually acceptable resolution to the dispute

Memo in Opposition - A memorandum in response to another written memorandum or written request to the court

Memorandum - A written document in support of a certain position

Merit Selection - A system for a judicial nomination commission to recommend candidates for judicial appointments to the governor

Mini-trial - A process in which each side presents its case to a neutral third party, usually one impartial advisor who has been selected by the litigants and their attorneys. Although the process resembles a trial, the presentation is abbreviated. Following the presentations, the parties' representatives meet, with or without the neutral third party, to negotiate a settlement

Misdemeanor - Offense less serious than a felony, punishable by a sentence other than being sent to prison (A.R.S. Section 13-105)

Modification Order - An order of the court that alters, changes, extends, amends, limits, or reduces an earlier order of the court

O

Oath - Swearing or affirming that a statement is true. If someone makes a statement under oath and knows it is false, that person may be subjected to prosecution for perjury. Written documents as well as spoken testimony may be made under oath

Obligee - Commonly refers to the person to whom monthly support is payable

Obligor - Commonly refers to the person ordered to pay support

Office of Child Support Enforcement (OCSE) - The federal office established to oversee the administration of Title IV-D of the Social Security Act

Offset - The reduction of a support-indebtedness (In IV-D, this refers to the application of federal or state tax refund monies to child support arrearage)

Opinion - Written statement issued to report the decision of an appellate court

Order to Show Cause/Order to Appear - A court order directing a person to appear in court and respond to a legal petition or complaint

P ─────────────────────────────

Parent/Child Contact - A court determination establishing the conditions under which a parent may be with his or her child; also known as Parenting Time.

Parentage - A determination that one person is the parent of a child and therefore is responsible for child support and may be entitled to parental rights and responsibilities and parent/child contact

Parental Rights and Responsibilities - (Used to be known as custody) Issues for court determination in a divorce or parentage action. Physical rights and responsibilities include where the child lives and who cares for the child; legal rights and responsibilities include the right to make decisions for the child, including granting permission for medical treatment for the child, and the right to have access to the child's school and medical records

Parenting Plan - A written document containing an agreement between parents indicating how a child will be raised and cared for after the parents separate or divorce. A written parenting plan is required whenever parents ask the court to order joint custody

Parenting Time - (See Parent/Child Contact in this Glossary). Once known as Visitation Party. A person who has appeared in court in regard to an action and whose rights are subject to the court's jurisdiction

Pass-Through - The amount of a collection, full or partial, which is paid to a custodial parent including the $50 TANF disregard

Paternity - A determination that establishes a man as the legal father of a child. Paternity must be established before a father may be entitled to parental rights, if the parents were never married

Payee - The person who receives the child support payments for the child. See: Oblige

Payment History - A printed statement of payments received by the court clerk or the support payment clearinghouse

Payor - The person ordered by the court to make child support payments. This is usually the parent who is not living with the child. See: Obligor Petit (Trial) Jury - The group of people selected to decide the facts and render a verdict in a civil or criminal trial

Petition - A formal written request filed with the Clerk of the Court requesting the court to take action

Petition for Review - An application asking an appellate court to examine a ruling or decision

Plaintiff - Someone who brings an action, such as a complaint

Plea - Response of a defendant to the criminal charges stated; the plea is usually "guilty" or "not guilty" Plea Agreement

Plea Bargain - A process between the accused and the prosecution to negotiate a mutually satisfactory outcome of the case

Pleading - The process by which parties file things in court, including beginning a case, responding to issues in court, and counterclaims. Eventually, only one or a few issues remain which the parties disagree on, and these are the issues that the court decides upon

Points of Law - The legal questions that a case may raise

Precinct - Geographic subdivision of city, town or county, used to describe the jurisdiction of a Justice of the Peace or for election purposes

Pre-Filing Conference - A meeting intended to resolve issues in lieu of court action

Preliminary Hearing - Court proceeding used to determine whether there is enough evidence against a person charged with a felony to proceed to trial

Presiding Judge - See Judge in this Glossary Probable Cause - Reasonable cause; there is more evidence for an argument than against it

Probation - A conditional suspension of the sentence given by a court in a criminal case. If the terms of probation are violated, probation may be revoked and the sentence carried out

Pro Bono Publico - "For the public good." When a lawyer takes a legal case without being paid and without expecting payment

Pro Per (Pro Se) - A Latin phrase meaning For oneself. A person appearing without benefit of an attorney, appearing for him/herself in court

Prosecutor - Attorney representing the citizens of a particular community or the state in a criminal case. This may be the city attorney, county attorney or attorney general

Pro Tem - A person appointed as a judicial officer on a temporary basis Putative Father - See: Alleged Father

R

Reciprocity/ Reciprocal - Denotes a relationship between states in which one extends the rights and privileges to citizens of another and vice versa

Record on Appeal - Those papers, transcripts and exhibits form the trial court that is forwarded to the appellate court for review

Recording a Judgment - The act of filing a certified copy of a judgment with a County Recorder in order to place a lien on any real property the judgment debtor may own in that county. Recording must be made in each county where the debtor may own property

Referral - Cases sent to the IV-D agency by various public assistance agencies to facilitate the collection of child and/or medical support so the aid recipient may become self-sufficient

Registration of an Order - A means of making an out-of-state child support order a State order under procedures set forth in the Revised Uniform Reciprocal Enforcement of Support Act

Registry - A section of the Office of Child Support that accepts child support payments and pays them to the custodial parent

Relief - The redress or assistance awarded to a plaintiff or petitioner by the court Remand - To send back; an appellate court may remand a case to the trial court for re-trial or other action

Reopen - Reopening of a case permits the introduction of new evidence and to permit a new trial

Request to Find - Request for written determination of facts by a judge after a trial

Respondent - The party who answers a complaint in a civil case or a party against whom an appeal is brought

Responding Jurisdiction - A county, district or state to which an interstate case is forwarded by the initiating jurisdiction for legal disposition

Responding State - See: Responding Jurisdiction Rest - A party is said to "rest" or "rest its case" when it has presented all of the evidence it intends to offer

Retention - The electoral process by which voters decide whether judges appointed by the governor will continue to serve another term in their current judicial capacity

Return of Service - A statement that a complaint or other document has been served on a party

Reverse - Decision of an appellate court to change all or part of the decision of a lower court

Review and Adjustment - In IV-D cases, a process to determine the appropriateness of the amount of support ordered to be paid and to change (modify) that amount to conform to state child support guidelines

RURESA - Revised Uniform Reciprocal Enforcement of Support Act: a statute adopted by most states to assist in the establishment and enforcement of support obligations when parents reside in different states

Modify - To alter; to change; to extend; to amend; to limit; to reduce

Motion - A request to a court for an order granting any kind of relief

N

Nisi Period - A period of time (usually 90 days) following a final divorce order during which neither party can marry again

Non-Custodial Parent (NCP) - The parent that has not been granted legal custody of the child; the parent who is not the primary caretaker of the child

Notary Public - A person who is legally authorized to administer oaths and verify that someone has completed an affidavit under oath

Notice of Appearance - A paper filed in court notifying the court and the other parties that a party (or their lawyer) is participating in the case. See Appearance in this Glossary

S

Satisfaction of Judgment - A document indicating a judgment has been paid or otherwise is no longer due, required to be filed with the clerk of each court where the judgment has been docketed and also recorded in the office of each county recorder where the judgment has been recorded

Sentence - Punishment set by the court or jury within the range of punishments authorized by statute

Separation Agreement - A document that may determine parental rights and responsibilities, parent/child contact and support without granting a divorce

Service or Service of Process - The formal delivery of a petition, notice, or other papers to a party in a legal action as prescribed by court rule

Settlement - An agreement that is reached by the opposing parties making it unnecessary for the court to resolve the controversy

Sheriff's Fee - The amount charged by the sheriff for serving a document to a party

Small Claims Court - A court that can decide on claims up to a certain, limited dollar amount. The proceedings are in the Justice of the Peace Court and are less formal than in other types of courts and parties usually represent themselves

Small Claims Division - Special division established within each justice of the Peace Court to legally resolve claims that do not exceed $2,500

Spousal Maintenance - Support for a spouse or former spouse ordered by the court; this arrangement may be temporary or permanent. In an IV-D case this can be enforced only when there is an accompanying child support order; also known as Alimony

State Parent Locator Service (SPLS) - The system in the IV-D agency used to locate parents

Status Conference - A meeting at court, in which the court attempts to identify what issues are contested, what discovery needs to be completed, and what future hearings are needed. No evidence is presented and no witnesses are called at these meetings

Statute - Law enacted by the Legislature and published in the State Revised Statutes

Statute of Limitations - Refers to the period of time within which a party must begin a legal action

Stipulation - An agreement between opposing parties on any matter relating to the proceeding or trial, such as an agreement on support, parental rights and responsibilities, parent/child contact and property division on either a temporary or final basis

Subpoena - An order to compel someone to come to a court at a certain date and time; there are penalties if that person doesn't come to court Suit - See Action in this Glossary

Summary Jury Trials - A process whereby a jury is selected, and counsel for each side in the dispute present their best case before the jury and judge. The jury is empanelled by the court, and at the conclusion of the presentations, the judge gives abbreviated instructions. The jurors return with an advisory verdict intended to educate the parties about the jury's view of the case. Counsel and parties are usually given an opportunity to discuss the basis for the advisory verdict with the jurors. A settlement conference is, then, conducted by the judge. If no settlement is reached, the parties may proceed to trial

Summons - A document directing a sheriff or other officer to notify the person named in the summons that a lawsuit has been started against him or her in court, and that he or she must go to court on the day listed in the summons and must file an answer to the complaint

Superior Court – This is trial court with a courthouse in each county. This court has jurisdiction over all criminal cases and over all civil cases involving a claim of more than $200. This court usually hears only civil cases

Supreme Court - The court of final appeal

T

Temporary Assistance for Needy Families (TANF) - A category of public assistance paid on behalf of children who are deprived of support by one or both of their parents due to disability, or continued absence (including desertion) from the home

Testimony - Statements made by witnesses who have taken an oath or affirmed that they will tell the truth

Transcript - Official written, word-for-word record of court proceedings

Trial - Formal presentation of facts to a court or jury in order to reach a legal decision

Trail De Novo - A re-trial of a case

True Bill - An indictment by a Grand Jury

U

Uniform Child Custody Jurisdiction Act (UCCJA) - All 50 states have this law, which ensures that only one state can decide parental rights and responsibilities of a particular child

Uniform Interstate Family Support Act (UIFSA) - Legislation designed to replace and improve upon

URESA Uncontested - A case in which all of the issues are resolved and agreed upon by all parties; usually the parties will file a stipulation and proposed order with the court

Un-reimbursable TANF - That amount of TANF monies expended for a family that is not recoverable because it exceeds the amount of support an obligor has been ordered by the court to pay. Example: Total TANF monies expended, $3,800 less Total due under child support order $2,000, equals a difference of $1,800

Uniform Reciprocal Enforcement of Support Act (URESA) - All 50 have this law, which is designed to assist people to receive child support from non-custodial parents living in other states

V

Vacated - A legal term meaning canceled or rescinded

Venue - The county or other geographical place in which a legal action is heard by the court

Verdict - Formal decision of a trial jury

Visitation - Now known as Parenting Time. See Parent/Child Contact in this Glossary   Voluntary Acknowledgment - A process by which parents can establish paternity without bringing a legal action

W

Wage Assignment/Order of Assignment - A court order directing an employer or other payor to withhold money (e.g., wages, earnings, interest or trust funds, unemployment insurance benefits, etc.) owed to a support obligor for payment toward a child support obligation   Wage

Withholding - A method of paying child support. Under court order, money is withheld from the wages of a non-custodial parent, sent to the Office of Child Support Registry and then sent to the custodial parent

Waiver - The intentional and voluntary relinquishment of a known legal right

Witness - Person who gives testimony regarding what he/she saw or heard

Writ - A document issued by a court which compels a sheriff or other officer to do something

ABOUT THE AUTHOR

There is no man more fitting of the description *"A Man On A Mission"* than Roderick Patterson, aka Sir Rod.

His positive outlook has awarded him tremendous success for many years. As a resident of Atlanta, GA, he has founded several organizations, such as the Sounds of Knowledge, a school-touring company, that visits local and regional schools, delivering positive messages to our youth, through the medium of music. Previously, Sir Rod headed one of the country's largest school assembly companies, Diversity Showcase Assemblies, where he spearheaded efforts that touched more than a million children across the nation. He has also worked as an art director for So-So Def Recordings, as well as Georgia Perimeter College. As an entertainer, artist, motivational speaker and new author, he believes his life to be a positive example to others, especially, young people. Currently, Sir Rod has published two self-motivating books, ***333 and Me… A Numbers Journey and 10 Commandments of The Stage… Make Them Remember You***, a top selling artist development book. Sir Rod, recently, founded Don't Bully, Inc., which is a non-profit company that operates as a community organization dedicated to empowering underserved children and communities by delivering anti-bullying and anti-drug educational assembly programs.

Sir Rod can be reached at http://www.sirrod.net

www.ingramcontent.com/pod-product-compliance
Lightning Source LLC
Chambersburg PA
CBHW071704040426
42446CB00011B/1906